Love Poems From Deep Within The Soul

ROBERT WORRALL

DEDICATION

I dedicate this book to my beautiful muse.

Robert Worrall

CONTENTS

ACKNOWLEDGMENTS

I wish to thank the heavenly angels, and all the people whose love inspires my poetry, and gives me inspiration.

Abracadabra! Love Just Realized

Abracadabra! I put a spell on you!
Red and pink, you love me so true.
Your heart will only, ever be for me
eyes of gold, and now you can see.

I light a red candle, and ask for you
as the pink glows, you know it too.
Not too much, just perfect of heart
a love that lasts, and never depart.

I say your name aloud, in my head
as I bind your heart, with this red.
Venus I ask, to bind this lady's soul
with this pink, our love will unroll.

With a piece, of your long dark hair
I visualize, a love we'll soon share.
On a candle, I've written your name
down it burns, till there's no flame.

Once again, I shout out your name
as this love for me, you proclaim!
Now the candles have burned out
your loving heart, is not in doubt.

I take up the pieces, and your hair
now in a bag, a secret, to ensnare.
Abracadabra! You are now, mine
the Goddess of love, will entwine.

All Alone

All alone! As I walk the streets in despair
I need some food, no money anywhere!
My feet are sore and my shoes in tatters
as nothing in my life, now! Really matters.

I move around a lot, as I haven't, a home
so tearful and depressed, as I'm all alone!
How did I end up in this terrible situation?
I found true love, before this degradation.

My clothes are ragged, and a little muddy
I have nothing left, and I haven't, a buddy.
My heart has left me, and all of my desire
without my true love, my life is really dire.

For the love we share, you've now denied
my soul is broken, and my dear! I've cried.
I can't believe! You ignore your own heart
and hide those feelings, and keep us apart.

Now my life, is surely turned upside down
I can't see a reason, to smile! I just frown!
Your face is, forever pictured, on my mind
as the love I have for you, is so, enshrined.

So I beg you! Take notice of your own soul
for we both need each other, to be whole.
I do need your heart and love to be shown
because without you, my hearts, all alone!

As Above, So Below

Love thy neighbour, love a good friend
love your foe, and everyone, to ascend.
When you find solace, in your own self
you will find happiness, and love, itself!

We forget that our planet needs us too
for all creatures, give it heart, to renew.
Without love, our planet, will surely cry
then it can say: life over, now goodbye!

Love is a power so strong, it changes all
without our love, we'll all be, sepulchral.
Left in gloom, and with no hope of love
all will pass, there'll be no, white dove.

Then, without the birds and those bees
there'll be no us, and no more enemies.
In truth, there'll be nothing left, to spoil
no human being and no animal, just soil.

Evolve your love and help out your soul
then your heart, will certainly be whole.
For love will show, as above! So below!
Heaven on Earth, we'll definitely know!

Bang, Bang, Love Hits

Bang, bang, my heart beats like a drum
you really make me feel, so very numb.
Bang, bang, my heart is so much on fire
your heart and love, is my only true desire.

Bang, bang, my heart does really need you
Cupid's arrow got me, before I had a clue.
Bang, bang, the middle of the heart it got
it really did, hit my one true, love hotspot.

Bang, bang, Cupid's arrow did get you too
I do think, our hearts were meant to pursue.
Bang, bang, we can't fight against our fate
we must surely, get together and celebrate.

Bang, bang, Fortune did give us a good hand
so we must really show, our love so grand.
Bang, bang, please let your heart out to me
then I will love, honour and cherish you see.

Bang, bang, now that's how fast love can hit
our hearts were never, meant to be separate.
Bang, bang, what can we certainly do now
apart from take our love vow, and say, wow!

Bang, bang, Heaven sent us on our love path
now we must follow, or face Heaven's wrath.
Bang, bang, just a guess, you know more or less
here it goes, I do profess, I love you, Jee! Yes!

Game of Love

You're dressed in pink and give me a wink
my heart is thumping, as my eyes do blink.
With a well defined face and gorgeous lips
my eyes all starry, and my heart now skips.

Your hazel eyes of gold, now sparkle at me
as my soul sees your soul, shouting yippee.
As your long dark hair, twinkles in the light
what a wonderful woman, my heart is right.

As I peep straight into your eyes, I see love
a true love in pure crystal, glancing hereof.
You know I'm looking, as you do turn away
but no sooner, you're gazing again, hooray!

While we're playing, a catch sight of game!
Your love's unveiled, as your hearts aflame.
As we're staring adoringly in this dark room
I do sense a sweet love, beginning to bloom.

We see and speak on many days thereafter
we give one another such fun, and laughter.
Our hearts were meant to be joined in love
we'll shout it out, from the rooftops above.

That Special Love

There is a love that many do not perceive
and some people just, cannot really believe.
This love I talk of can be very impolite
yes it's that very special, love at first sight.

This is what happened, about eight years ago
when I met a lady, with a beautiful glow.
I did not believe, these things could occur
but when I saw her, my heart did, simply purr.

She was just standing there in the sunlight
looking so beautiful, my heart was alight.
I had no courage, at that moment to speak
all I could do, was look at this lady so chic.

The years went by, my heart did just wait
was this "love at first sight", really our fate.
Destiny stepped in like a spiralling hurricane
that beauty I'd seen, I had now found again.

Now I am not sure whether our love can be
but whatever fate decides, will be the key.
All I can say is that our love is long overdue
maybe; one day soon, she'll say; I love you.

So now you know that love at first sight
does really happen, and is a lovely delight.
When this special love does transpire
just let your heart, follow the fire.

Portrait of a Lady

She's like a painting a complete work of art
this woman I love, who has taken my heart.
Her lips are painted red and gentle to touch
with a kiss so wonderful, I love her so much.

She sits on her chair, in a pose, so eloquent
her face is smiling, as she does look elegant.
As her golden eyes are painted, as luminous
as they exhibit her beauty and gracefulness.

Her long dark hair just shimmers in the light
as I'm the artist, using a radiant, candlelight.
Her dress is long, and painted, in pure white
it's so virtuous, but this painting does excite.

The background is unlit and painted in black
this lady's so intriguing, she looks right back.
This lady I adore, is clasping a pink bouquet
some flowers I did give her, earlier that day.

Now the paintings finished and starts to dry
as she comes over to look, she begins to cry!
"That's beautiful" she says, a poem in paint
well! I do love you completely, then I faint!!

Book of Fates Love

I've found this ancient book, to evaluate
with secrets of love, as destined by fate.
That can only open, with a true love key
what's that! As I ponder, what it may be.

I wonder what this could, possibly mean
by accident I drop it, now a clue is seen.
With a heart of love, and by a real name
this Book of Fates love, can open, again.

I say aloud the name of the lady, I adore
with luck it might open, so I can explore.
Well! I didn't really believe, that it would
but now it has, I'm wondering if I should.

As I open the book, and look at the index
it does really mirror, some type of codex.
Searching for my name, I peer at the book
I flick through, it opens on a page, I look!

Mmmm, there it is! Standing out, in bold
now that is weird, I think! If truth be told.
To read the page, I need to be very brave
as it may tell me something, I don't crave.

Do I? Or don't I? Read this part about me
as this book, is Fates own way, to foresee.
However! I do have a strong urge, to look
and read what it says for me, in this book.

I do glance to see, if something stands out
and I see a woman's name, it does shout.
It says; a woman I love, does love me also
true love will happen, only after, the woe.

I shut the book, after reading this extract
for I'm scared, and wonder how to react.
I did see, that I was supposed to mention
"just say; dreams of another dimension".

Actually knowing, our love is fates decree
gives me heart, as our love is a guarantee.
Joining our hearts and souls, is divine will
and I'm sure our love, will certainly thrill

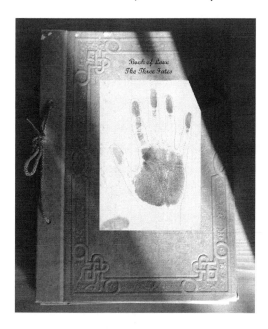

Bring Love to the World

Love is the best thing in the world today
money is not needed, just a heart, I say.
What would our lives be, without a heart
boring and horrible, it would tear us apart.
With the love, we have all got deep inside
world peace, we could achieve, with pride.
I know there are those, who are heartless
we really need to pull together, regardless.

The problem with people, in society today
they couldn't care less, they just runaway.
If we all did that, then why give to charity
money surely, can't stop, your unpopularity.
All the money in the world, cannot buy heaven
for it is a place, for those who have, love given.
So what must you do, to survive in your life?
Give out love to all, and not that pitiful strife!

Now here's the challenge, give love a chance
open your heart, move forward, and dance.
Listen to your heart, your world will improve
and everyone around you, will surely approve.
Well it's time to send out, our love to everyone
so spread the word, via my poem, to anyone.
Pass the beauty of love, on to those who need
give out love to all, and not hate, and greed.

It does apply, to animals and wildlife, as well
for we all need love, so we can perfectly gel.
Please give out the same love, to all creatures
our loving hearts, really should, be the teachers.
Remember to love, love, love and love
bring peace, peace, peace from above.
Make a start now, and send your heart
Heaven is watching, now become part.

Celestial Light of Love

My heart is pounding and my head is spinning
for this woman I love, does keep me grinning.
She is so gorgeous my eyes show tears of joy
as the angels of heaven, tell us, please enjoy!

When I close my eyes, she is all that I can see
I'm fixated by her beauty, and her aura, for me.
The sparkle in her eyes, is like, a celestial light
sent from Heaven, like some kind of meteorite.

To this woman, the whole of my life is devoted
as the sun and moon, celestial hearts denoted.
Without her love, my inner light will never grow
she's my ambience, together, our star will glow.

She lights up my soul, with her heart of flames
her heart needs mine, this love, she proclaims.
Two solitary, celestial lights which become one
this true love of ours, shines forth, like the sun.

My love, now remembers why she came here
as our souls together, are a heavenly sphere.
This light we produce emits rays, of sunshine
as this star of ours, creates a true love shrine.

Words of Love

God! Behold,
I write these words of love to you my sweet
a letter for a love, so wonderful and complete.
That first time I saw you, my heart was taken
for your beauty before me, just left me shaken.

Your heart spoke, with a harmonious melody
that left my heart and soul, in perfect parody.
I could do nothing at all, but look and stare
my eyes were dazzled, by an allure so rare.

Such beauty I could never, have dreamt about
till that day I met you, I was then in no doubt.
You were sent from Heaven, we're meant to be
our spirits as one, forever in accord, for all eternity.

Our lives have been drawn, together more and more
since that day, our hearts and souls, couldn't ignore.
I know, you get the same feelings and dreams as me
destiny and fortune, leave nothing to chance you see.

So what must happen, in our wonderful love, now
our Guardian Angels, will come to help us, go wow!
They're the ones, who will leave nothing to chance
so that, our love will forever be, in balance.

Darling I Send You a Flower

Darling lady I've sent you a flower today
so it will be delivered, in God's own way.
This wonderful flower is perfect like you
it carries my heart, and so much love too.

God has sent a message from me before
another person, so warned you, to ignore.
Listen to your heart and love you will find
for this love of ours, Heaven sent to bind.

This message of love is a sign you'll know
for a sweet lady, whose heart is on show.
All that love which is hidden in your soul
you must set free, it's written in a scroll.

God! Behold this message of love for you
my true love, you'll understand this clue.
This fabulous pink brightens up your day
a bouquet of flowers, your love will stay.

Time to say and open up your true heart
this love of ours, is impressive and smart.
Heaven acknowledges our loving powers
and sent down Angels, and those flowers.

Darling, Sweet Darling

Darling, sweet darling, my one true desire
you're such a pretty lady, and truly on fire.
Darling, sweet darling, I love you, so much
my heart is yours, as my soul you touched.

Your true inner beauty does glow so bright
you are an angel, sent from Heaven, right!
As I gaze at you, I can see your hearts, love
a beauty of nature, just as white, as a dove.

You glow with a radiance that gives delight
to everything around you, you're so, polite.
With hair so blonde, it matches, your heart
and the clothes you wear, white and smart.

With a sweet soft voice so pleasant to hear
my soul is pure, with your music, to my ear.
As you don't realize, my inspiration, is clear
it's you! My darling, sweet darling, it's you!

You're the one who makes me so complete
and the real reason, my poetry, is so sweet.
I think of you, each time I write my rhymes
darling, sweet darling, my lady who chimes.

Divine Love Spark

Intense and acute your mind is absolute
those eyes are sleepy, and really weepy.
Look into your mind and see me in there
for I am your love, and instantly you care.

Those eyes are heavy you're feeling tired
my soul you seek, for our love is required.
Heartfelt and acute your mind is absolute
deep within your heart, you feel destitute.

For my loving heart is your one true desire
our pure love, will make your soul perspire.
Deeper and deeper into your heart you go
to find this love, which heaven did bestow.

Now heavy and sleepy you're ever so deep
those eyes are closed, you can't now peep.
At the centre you find your heart and soul
but now you know, I will make you whole.

You're now in a trance and a dreamy state
as this love we share, you begin to elevate.
You open your mind's eye and see my face
as this love you've found, you do embrace.

You hear a beep and you begin to awaken
as you remember, your heart is now taken.
You've found your inner self, and true love
sent to you, by a divine spark, from above.

Blonde Woman Sweet and Divine

Blonde woman, so sweet and divine
a beautiful smile, you're so sublime.
Always lovely and certainly amazing
I totally love you, my heart is blazing.

Those glittering blue eyes, I do adore
there like diamonds, lovely and pure.
When I gaze, at your fabulous red lips
my eyes do open, my heart, just skips.

Your figure is so faultless, and lovable
so much style, you're surely adorable.
No woman, is better looking than you
my eyes only, see such beauty, so true.

My heart is lonely, I need your caress
I should open up, decide and confess.
This love I keep hidden, so deep inside
you're too good for me, I'm petrified.

I don't know, if my emotions do show
your kiss I need, under the mistletoe.
You are an angel, my gorgeous honey
please my sweet, be my Easter bunny.

Fairytale Love

Why have you started to hide away from me!
My heart does crumble, when you, I can't see.
Your heart loves me, like my heart, loves you
time for you to open up, let our love, through.

You've tried to show, that love for me, before
so why now hide, and pretend, you're not sure.
I can see it in your honey eyes, when you look
our love is so intended, it's like a fairytale book.

I've missed seeing your beauty, so far this week
my heart prays that before the end, you speak.
Jee, yes! My heart, needs your loving heart now
the angels know, that I've made a true love vow.

I've given everything to you my beautiful sweet
you're like a gift, heaven sent, a wonderful treat.
My heart, my soul, my life, everything I give to you
please let me know now, that you love me too.

Not long left before, my heart is a complete mess
without you, I'll be in complete and utter distress.
I need you to tell me sooner, rather than later
listen to your heart, the angels and the Creator.

I would like to thank you, my darling, in advance
for taking my heart, and giving me a real chance.
I love you so much, my life is in a desperate spin
please now, tell me, and let our love, begin.

Fire of Passion

Alone in the dark, as I'm thinking of you
my eyes are so teary, my love is so true.
The fire does flicker as my heart shakes
all those tears now, making a great lake.

I wish that we could be, together tonight
for my love for you, is so pure and bright.
My heart can only see, the beauty of you
I wish my dream, would really come true.

You're kind and gentle, pretty and polite
I'm truly devoted, you are such a delight.
Gorgeous long dark hair and eyes of gold
for you my lady, I'll do anything, I'm told.

I couldn't describe the love I have for you
a love this good, must always rendezvous.
I'm still sat, by the fire, in a perfect dream
eyes are closed, as my heart does scream.

My heart now is broken, as I begin to drift
my soul is leaving me, I need your love gift.
Please my darling, stop those tears of mine
show your love for me, which is truly divine.

Open your eyes, to see your heart, in plight
your soul is teary, it's time to make it, right.
Please! Don't let that love you have subside
let out the passion, and feed the fire, inside.

Friday 13th Love

Well it's Friday the 13th and my luck is in
my pretty lady, will show her love within.
Her heart she will open, for me this day
my luck is in, I really, don't have to pray.

Jeez! Her love will shout out, you see
because her heart now, is surely for me.
Friday 13th what a lovely, lucky number
Fate has caused, our true love, thunder.

Unlucky it never will be, for you and me
as it will become, our love anniversary.
Freya, the lady of love, in Norse tradition
will help us through, our love, transition.

Abracadabra, our love is now to start
with lucky number thirteen, at its heart.
The last thing left to say; is from me to you
you're so sweet, hun! Now, say you do!

God! Behold, True Love

Fate has chosen that gorgeous woman for me
our destiny, is written in the sky for all to see.
The god of love, Eros, did speak from above
and said; "just success", can come from our love.

This divine decree, heaven sent to you and me
God! Behold, this true love he meant to be.
Our Guardian Angels do work, to make our fate so
chance and karma, they come and help to bestow.

What a wonderful thing our destiny really is
nothing can stop this sweet chaos of bliss.
Our lives together, in the stars of the universe
brought to life in this beautiful poetry verse.

Nothing in our fortunate existence, is a coincidence
everything we do know, is made purely by influence.
So what can we both do to help our true love along
if you sit down my dear, I'll sing you a beautiful song.

You are my love; you are my love,
the one I do adore
come to me, come to me
and let me be your amour.

You are my love; you are my love,
the one I do cherish
come to me, come to me,
our love will never perish.

God Given Love

I walk and walk in a forest of love
as I hear a sound, I look up above.
It is an Angel coming down to me
sent from Heaven, about my plea.

As this Angel came to the ground
so many lights, shining all around.
He spoke to me through my mind
God heard, the prayer you signed.

He said to me, you made this vow
God accepts! your love he'll allow.
When the next full moon is bright
your lover's heart, will truly ignite.

She'll see your face in her dreams
her heart just for you, as it beams.
Nothing else will she desire in life
except her wish, as your new wife.

How will I know, this vision is true?
When this woman says, I love you!
She will send you her loving heart
then you'll know, God! did impart!

God Said it's True

Foxy lady so gorgeous and amazing
you're so beautiful, my eyes glazing.

This fantastic love that I have found
you're a princess that does astound.

Loves true kiss has already occurred
by Cupid's arrow, a love transferred.

Those hazel eyes of crystal foretold
this love we now share, God behold.

My love for you is absolutely sincere
as you're a lady, I undeniably revere.

I look at you as my soul does bounce
for our sweet love, please announce.

Without this love our hearts will cry
Heaven gave this love, to you and I.

The truth is hidden from your heart
the love you have, will never depart.

My heart is yours and my soul is too
I love you so much, God said it's true.

Goddess, Goddess

Goddess, Goddess! You're truly divine
already you know! I'll make this rhyme.
You nurture the Earth and all the souls
for we overlook, our true hearts goals.

You have taught us to love each other
as you are our kind, Universal Mother.
Most of your guidance we now ignore
and really don't listen, to you anymore.

Your heart and soul is put into woman
but! Man has usurped this loving plan.
So delightful, honest, wise, and loving
you are the one, who is so all knowing.

A woman gives love to us at the start
as life moves, we fall away and depart.
We forget all that love formed at birth
from the Goddess, who gave us worth.

Goddess, Goddess! You send us a sign
helping us all with love, you are divine.
Goddess, Goddess! We take! You give
you help us live, so please do forgive!

My Heart is Incomplete

My heart is incomplete, it is missing a section
your heart it does need, to make it perfection.
Without this piece of you, my heart can never rest
for it is also a part of me, and my life's, true quest.

So now you see, I can never be truly complete
until the day our hearts, can fit together so neat.
I am missing your love, that was really intended
please my love, come and make us, so splendid.

My soul is in need of you, I know, yours does too!
For they are a part, and must always rendezvous.
Our souls have always been together, somehow!
For it is our destiny, we have made a solemn vow.

If we don't join together, our hearts will feel alone
Chaos will reign about us, our souls will then groan.
Fortune and Fate, can never allow this catastrophe
they'll join our hearts, and save us from our tragedy.

My love, all I ask of you, is for you to give me a clue
or let me know, that you really do love me, so true.
So that we can once again, find our true happiness
in this life, as we have before, and will again, I guess!

Heartfelt Plight

Raindrops are falling from the sky
like the tears rolling down my eye.
Why! Oh Why! Does my heart cry
for this lady, but I don't know why!

I had a vision of a little girl at night
she asked for help, with her plight.
Her mum needed my help she said
those words did fill me, with dread.

Over and over she cried out to me
my hand she pulled, for me to see.
This little girl I could not recognize
as the tears filled up, both my eyes.

After what seems like a long night
the girl did finally, fade from sight.
I'm so anxious and distressed now
why had she come to me anyhow!

I had a weird feeling she was mine
her mum my wife, in another time.
It's like they were grieving over me
and this was her last heartfelt plea.

I've not had a vision again like this
but I do realize something's amiss.
I still see a girls face from that night
and that real loving heartfelt plight.

Hearts Connected

I search for a woman, my soul detected
a woman so nice, our hearts connected.
Our souls were expected, to reconvene
as lucky for her, is that number thirteen.

As this number will align our two hearts
for mine is the same, my name so smart.
When both our thirteen's, do intertwine
our souls in concert, are pure crystalline.

Long blonde hair, that shows her beauty
her stunning face, does make her a cutie.
She is rather tall with a figure so slender
a gorgeous voice, that is soft and tender.

Her cute blue eyes so pure and hypnotic
will make my heart, bizarre and chaotic.
Her lips are red and certainly astounding
my head spins and my heart is pounding.

What I need! Is for her soul to find mine
then our souls, have discovered a shrine.
For our hearts were lost in a time before
now I've seen you, our love can restore!

Heavenly Love

It's party time as our souls combine
a seductive lady, with a love design.
A glowing brunette with lips so nice
kisses me tonight, its love paradise.

Her love she whispers down my ear
Oh what a woman! She has no fear.
I have prayed for this love we share
you are my dearest, I'm now aware.

The love I see in her cute hazel eyes
now that is, an astounding surprise!
I always felt that she did love me so
but I didn't think, she'd let me know.

As I'm looking straight into her eyes
I see her charm, she does hypnotize.
So completely devoted to her, am I!
I'd give my life for hers, I will not lie.

It's party time and our vows are said
time for our dance, now we're wed.
So party with us and have lots of fun
for the love we have, is Heaven spun.

Hidden Tears

I whisper my words of true love, to you
you cannot hear it, for it's now a taboo!
I love you, I love you, my heart is yours!
Forever and ever as my love, just pours.

I yearn and pray for your beautiful soul
for I love you so much, I'm in a big hole.
My soul is lonely, for your love it needs
until you respond, my heart still bleeds.

You do love me, your feelings are there
as Heaven states, you will soon declare.
Those eyes of yours, have hidden tears
so crystal clear, are your true love fears.

I know it's difficult, our love just shines
as now your dreams, give you the signs.
Listen to your heart, and hear your soul
for my love, is your souls, one true goal.

So whisper to me, and let your love out
I'll listen carefully, for I'm truly, devout.
When you can express your love for me
then our souls will be happy, and free!

Hopeless Love

My heart is true I really love you
it's perfectly set, to truly pursue.
You are so perfect, a true delight
for I love you, you are quite right.

I am so lonely without your heart
for a lovers dart, did tear it apart.
Such a woman with beautiful hair
long and dark, it's certainly unfair.

The desire I have I hide within me
you're too cute, I know it you see.
I don't believe this love will begin
all I know is! To get out the violin!

Out of this world and ever so nice
I definitely need, heavenly advice.
It doesn't matter what I do or say
I do need your loving heart today.

You're a lady from a real fairytale
with no happy ending, as I do fail.
I will love you till the end of time
as my poem, one day we'll rhyme.

I Adore You

I really need my beautiful love with me
my heart is sad and lonely without thee.
I will always see the beauty within you
no matter what your heart, ever does do.

I wish I could let you know the way I feel
but I am too shy, so my heart I can't reveal.
You know that I really do, love you so much
you are shy too, but please, do get in touch.

My heart and soul, have given you their all
but I just seem, to have hit a large brick wall.
I know in your heart, your love is real and true
but there really is nothing, more that I can do.

My heart is lost; I'm stuck in the mist of love
I can't escape, without some help from above.
I ask those guardian angels to help my heart
for now I need you, my loving sweetheart.

They said to me; look up at the clouds, to see
she does love you, we can surely guarantee.
Her heart is true, but she does have doubts
but before too long, you'll hear her shouts.

My love I have for you, is surely one of a kind
your heart and soul, is so beautifully defined.
The elegance, that surrounds you, is so pure
so perfect you are, I can't help it, I do adore.

I Hypnotize You

Look into my eyes, as I can hypnotize
your mind is mine, you now visualize.
Look into my eyes, as you see a stone
pure and clear, it's a crystal unknown.

Look into my eyes, as you feel so tired
your mind is weary, and now, rewired.
Look into my eyes, and see the crystal
it's really so clear, and certainly vestal.

Look into my eyes, you're heart is true
you love me so much, you certainly do.
Look into my eyes, and see the beauty
you notice me, and think what a cutie.

Look into my eyes, as you feel excited
your heart is fast, you're so delighted.
Look into my eyes, and see them spin
faster and faster, as your soul gives in.

Look into my eyes, as you spin in time
faster and faster, as our souls do align.
Look into my eyes, from blue to green
faster and faster, my love you've seen.

Look into my eyes, and open up yours
awaken your soul, as it then reassures.
Wake up, wake up and see a pink rose
one you wished, as our love you chose.

I love You So Much

Chorus
I love you so much, yes I certainly do
I love you so much, my heart is true.
I love you so much, I really need you
please sweet lady, say; you do, too!

My soul is yours and your soul is mine
for our love is pure, excellent and fine.
You love me so, I see it in those eyes
this beautiful love, you do recognize.

Chorus
My heart you hit with a love so bright
true love it is, such a heavenly delight.
As you walk past and look into my eye
I'm all yours, as you sing a cute lullaby.

Chorus
Lovely dark hair that passes your neck
for goodness sake, I'm an utter wreck.
I can't cope without your love my dear
for my heart sees, a woman to revere.

Chorus
This beautiful love from a previous life
has followed us, I need you as my wife.
Those eyes of gold that sparkle at me
a husband is what, you want from me.

Chorus
I love you so much, yes I certainly do
I love you so much, my heart is true.
I love you so much, I really need you
please sweet lady, say; you do, too!

I'm So Lucky

Twinkle, twinkle, glimmer and shine
a flutter a wink, your eyes see mine.
Sparkle, sparkle, a flicker and a blink
glisten and glitter, our eyes interlink.

Glitz and glamour, you dress so nice
you're so wonderful, I'm in paradise.
Eyes of pure gold, that enlighten me
shiver and quiver, my heart set free.

Fun and games, my hearts in flames
you dilly-dally, your heart, proclaims.
Kiss and a cuddle, I'm in real trouble
as your heart does, begin, to bubble.

Sing; Sing our love is pure and strong
as our two hearts, will sing our song.
Do-wah-diddy, diddy-dum-diddy-do
such a gorgeous lady, I sure love you.

Do-wah-diddy diddy-dum-diddy-dee
allow your heart, to open up for me.
Ding-Dong! As you go down the aisle
I'm so lucky, with a big grin and smile.

A love Like This

A bolt of lightning strikes my head
as a lovable lady walks past, in red.
She looks at me, and I see her face
what a beauty, my heart does race.

I can't believe it's happened to me
love at first sight, I did not foresee.
Closer she gets she begins to speak
now I'm trembling, knees all weak!

Hello! She says, our eyes do meet
I nod my head, my voice obsolete.
We agree to have a chat and drink
at a nearby cafe, as I see her wink.

She tells me she has fallen for me
an instant love, she didn't foresee.
Now I tell her, I feel the same way
she then says, this love we'll obey.

A couple of years, have passed by
we are still together, we did unify.
Happily married, with a baby due
a love like this, can happen to you!

It's My Love! Hurray

The moon is out and the stars are bright
not a cloud in the sky, I'll dream tonight.
It's really quiet as I lie down on the lawn
I look up to the skies, as I let out a yawn.

As I gaze at the twinkling stars up above
I start to dream, about the woman I love.
The woman I see with her long dark hair
and those hazel eyes, which do ensnare.

I can see her cute face, within my dream
what a beautiful woman, she is supreme.
As I gaze, I notice, her eyes watching me
this can't happen! It's my dream you see.

It's not long before she shouts my name
as she says, "Our dreams are the same".
I test her out, and ask! How can this be?
"You love me, as I love you too! Agree".

As we talk, I start to hear birds tweeting
she says she'll call, to arrange a meeting.
My dream is fading, and so is my sweet
I'm waking up, from this dream so neat.

Don't go! Don't go! As I shout out to her
what a shame! As my mind is a total blur.
As I wake up, I can see it's a glorious day
as the phone rings, it's my love! Hurray!

Love Eyes

With such gorgeous eyes you did realize
we'd synchronized, as you hear my cries.
Then we harmonize as you do hypnotize
with hazel eyes our love did, materialize.

The Fates devise, as our love intensifies
as I'm paralyzed by your gorgeous eyes.
Your heart will rise, with a cute surprise
as you hear my sighs, as my poetry cries.

With highs and lows our hearts energize
as our love amplifies, as you do visualize.
Those cries of love as your heart justifies
will equalize, our hearts now synthesize.

Lets finalize what this true love signifies
remove your guise, as our love does rise.
Don't theorize; open up those cute eyes
no more whys! Or lies! Just those, sighs!

Our love satisfies you as it's no surprise
as I idolize, and love you, my lady arise!
Publicize your love, as it now magnifies
organize, and let out, those loving cries.

Love in the Sky

Your name is in the clouds above
written so clearly, just like a dove.
The sun does shine ever so bright
just like a flame, our hearts ignite.
A gust of wind is sent into the sky
like a whirlwind, our love is nigh.

As this day moves slowly to night
the setting sun, is quite the sight.
Night arrives as the darkness falls
in your dreams, my love just calls.
As all the stars twinkle and glisten
to your dream, you must so listen.

An adorable owl is what you hear
Goddess Athena, is certainly near.
Proof our hearts must surely share
truth of your love, so do be aware.
As you're awoken from this dream
your true love, will certainly gleam.

From this day on our souls are one
our hearts in love, life's just begun.
This love of ours is simple and true
my stunning princess, I do love you.
I know your heart is definitely clear
Cupid's arrow, did certainly appear.

Love Muddle (Distress)

My words today are a deep, deep, riddle
but my sweet lovely one, is in the middle.
I have used them ever so sloppy, I guess!
A jay is what I need, to make my true bliss.

Well what more of a muddle can I do now
oh yes; my love life, is really in need of Tau.
The woman of my dreams is so wonderful
I must look, completely and utterly pitiful.

My heart and soul are bound to you my dear
the love I have, suddenly may become clear.
I know you wonder what I really do think
but look at this poem, my heart is in sync.

It is time to re-arrange our lives, you and me
just guess, and maybe, you will really now see.
It's all there for you, my heart, my soul, my life
without you there's nothing, please! Be my wife.

So now you see, you really are everything to me
I would do anything for you, my darling beauty.
You are the one part of me, that I am still missing
now all I need from you is maybe, some kissing.

This really is my code written in this dodgy ode
will she now, be able to understand and decode.
I really am an enigma that you have left in a mess
my heart is confused, I am in love distress.

Love Tragedy

My life is a tragedy and I have no hope
there is no laughter, my heart can't cope.
What I need right now, is some jubilation?
Some type of love letter, or love dedication.

Sad and lonely is what my heart does feel today
for I need my love so much, I must sit and pray.
Oh God! What did I do! To have fate like this!
That makes my love life completely amiss?

The woman I wish and pray for at night, yes, you!
You're the woman I love, so beautiful and true.
You are the only one, I undoubtedly need now
I guess, I must learn to show you somehow.

I am not good looking, and you are so beautiful
what can I do! That can make me look suitable.
That's an impossibility I really do need a miracle
for our love to shine, and make it reciprocal.

I really am in tears my heart is broken in two
I love you so much my dear, I just can't tell you!
My heart would really love, to hear you say to me
I love you, I want to be your fiancée.

Lovers Song

Ding Dong, Ding Dong
I'll sing you a song about a lady
who made my heart belong
Ding Dong, Ding Dong,
I'll sing you a song about our hearts
they'll always sing along.

My wonderful lady
with the long dark hair, I love you my sweet
but you're not aware.
I need your love so our hearts can attach
sweet, sweet lady
they are a true match.

Your eyes of love
that sparkle in the light, send out those signals
like a love satellite.
The feelings inside you must now let out
sing and dance
and your heart will shout.

An exquisite face
and a figure so stunning, my loving heart
just can't stop drumming.
Your love for me, is burning you up inside
let it out, let it out
and become my bride.

Let's sing and dance
for a lovers romance, now take my hand
so our love can dance.
So sing along to this sweet little song
our love belongs
Ding Dong, Ding Dong.

My Heart is Calling

A woman so pure kind and tender
you're so stunning, I do surrender.
Hair so black it sparkles in the sun
it looks so soft, it's heavenly spun.
Skin so light your eyes are distinct
I'm in a trance, as you just winked.

You're so dainty just like a figurine
curves so good, a Goddess is seen.
A cute pink dress and you do shine
as twinkling eyes, make you divine.
Like a crystal, you're pure of heart
please allow, our true love to start.

I'm tearful and lonely without you
my eyes so red, my heart just blew.
Inside your eyes I can see true love
but what we need, is a little shove.
I pass my days wishing only for you
and wondering if, your love is true.

One day I hope our love will beam
then we'll make, the perfect team.
A glowing love for everyone to see
for our hearts, will certainly agree.
All I can say to you now, my darling
is! I love you! My heart is calling!

My Heart Needs You Here

As the sun shines and a stormy wind does blow
I'm drifting through time, and space you know!
I feel so hot and my body seems like electricity
as I've hit the centre space, I'm pure negativity.

Am I now here? Or am I somewhere different?
I couldn't say it's like a rainbow, so magnificent.
My eyes now glowing as I pick a time and place
for goodness sake! It's certainly like a fireplace.

I'm feeling exhausted as I go past the mid-point
I hope I find my love, and it doesn't, disappoint.
There's a light up ahead which I'm sent towards
I pass through it and fall onto some floorboards.

Is this the right place and the correct time zone?
Will she remember me? Or, will I be, unknown?
I can see her stood looking over me on the floor
as I tell her I'm so tired, and my head really sore.

The next thing I remember is her waking me up
giving me a glass of water, and telling me to sup.
Then she's says to me; how did you get in here
I ask where am I, she's says; my dream my dear.

Ohh what is this! Time travel it should've been
in your dream! I'm unsure what this, will mean.
I know she says: As I wished you to me my dear
as I love you so true, my heart needs you here!

Sweet Dream

I had a dream this past week, that my love so sweet
had something to show me, ever so beautiful and neat.
Friends and colleagues saw this present she had for me
"How beautiful that really is" they said "where is he".

"Outside" is the reply that came from another friend
but by that time, I had gone inside to hide and pretend.
You see I heard, everything that was said inside that room
as I was stood outside, listening, and trying not to assume.

Before I could hide away, a friend of hers told me "stay"
my true love then came to me and opened a box, okay.
No more of this dream did I see that night to my dismay
what a disappointment it was, to have such a short foray.

I know this dream is one that you have been able to view
this dream is really our fate that we foresaw, and just new.
What must we do? Clearly we must now take that chance
so that our love can finally advance.

This poem is to tell you how a dream, can turn into reality
sometimes they're our future foreseen, and not just triviality.
So pay close attention to whatever you see in your sleep
as this could become something real that you keep.

Robert Worrall

Please, Please, I Love You

Yet again! I'm up real early and cannot sleep
I love you so much my darling, I just weep.
My heart and soul don't have any direction
all I can do, is sit and wait, for your affection.

I can't stop thinking, how beautiful you are
truly your gorgeous, you're my superstar.
My hope is, that one day your love I'll see
and then maybe, we'll be together in glee.

The pain I have, and the sickness I now feel
is truly because, my love for you is so real.
Every time, I think of you, tears will ensue
my heart is cold and blue, I really love you!

I know that you wish to be my loving bride
so why not say, rather than, pray and hide.
Yes, things are always difficult at the start
we must both listen, and open up our heart.

If we do not learn, to listen to our inner soul
all we will have left, in our heart, is a big hole.
Please, Please, Please I need your love today
Please, Please, I love you, I need you to say.

Pink and Red heart

Our hearts are one, you and me
always and forever they will be.
Our hearts, beat in perfect time
the love we share, is so sublime.

Our minds, are of the same kind
they will forever, be so entwined.
Our thoughts are for each other
you really are the complete lover.

Our lives together, for all eternity
nothing can stop us, you and me.
The love we share is so supreme
nothing else, is there in our dream.

The twinkle in your eyes, I can see
three times, I saw your love plea.
I can tell from the words you say
you love me, just the same way.

You know together we should be
so open your heart, and talk to me.
It's as easy as doing your A,B,C.
just talk to me, you will then see.

Our love of nature, a jay I guess
will open your heart to success.
Listen carefully, to what I've said
now it's time for pink and red.

Our Hearts Do Sing

My head is in the clouds this day
and my eyes seeing, stars above.
You know my heart is in disarray
for you're so nice, the one I love.

I close my eyes as I see your face
you I cherish, the woman I adore.
So much beauty and full of grace
those eyes of gold, I can't ignore.

I await that moment you tell me
your heart is right, I do love you.
At that moment my eyes will see
angels of light, for a love so true.

In a white dress you are amazing
my heart is racing, you're so nice.
I look at you, my eyes are glazing
the woman I love, I'm in paradise.

I take thee to be my wedded wife
and I give my heart, with this ring.
Our love is pure and for all our life
as loving souls, our hearts do sing.

Poem of Love

What can I say to my beautiful lady today?
I do not have any words, just a bouquet.
Pink and red, flowers of a rhyme I did write
what now, will you send me out this night.

Will you send me a message of true love
or send your heart on a pure white dove.
I can see, you really wish to let me know
it's time now, for that true heart to show.

My problem is that I feel, I'm doing wrong
even if, my heart and soul are truly on song.
Your eyes do show that your love is strong
and that our hearts, so close, surely belong.

The signals I gave out, you did understand
what I need now, is your sweet loving hand.
Right now, your heart does yearn and ache
send your affection, your dream I can make.

I'm Sorry for the heartache I have generated
but I'm the same, my heart is so frustrated.
We need to sort out, those feelings for sure
then our love for each other, will be secure.

I make my move just like a game of chess
you are the one I really love so true, I guess.
I'm so sorry for my heart, I need you for joy
but when I see you, I just feel so shy and coy.

The words I write are always done for you
I cannot do this, for anyone else you know.
My heart and soul is in my poems my sweet
without you my love, they become obsolete.

You're Beautiful

My life now will never ever, be the same
now that I've found, my true love again.
My heart and soul, are on a sweet isle
while your mind, does keep you in denial.

Your heart and soul, they tell you the truth
but that mind of yours, ignores the proof.
Listen to your heart, then you will foresee
that heaven did plan, our love, surely to be.

Fate has decided to bring us back together
as our love is meant to be, forever and ever.
Another life, a solemn vow our hearts made
that our love, will be, our only life's crusade.

I know the timing is off, and Chaos will reign
but our love is so pure, it will never wane.
Our love is so supreme, it can never deviate
made in Heaven, our love does reciprocate!

Well my beauty with the sweet blue eyes
you certainly do make my heart hit the skies.
Just one thing, I have to say to you my deary
you're beautiful! My heart's gone all teary!

The Lady in Black

I see a fine woman, dressed all in black
she's so spellbinding, I'm an insomniac.
Her voice is soft, and lovely at all times
as she talks so nice, I only hear rhymes

She's ever so smart with a caring mlnd
such a radiant skin, her face is defined.
Hair so long and dark, just as her dress
a captivating woman, with true finesse.

My heart is lured with a voice so sweet
I stare into space, with a look of defeat.
As a Siren, she's singing to lure my soul
I scream so loud, as my soul does unroll.

So what can I do? I'm under, her power
she sees I love her, as I call her a flower.
I've lost my heart, for she still won't say
I love you! Let's love, honour and obey!

She's taken my heart and taken my soul
I do need help for our love, to be whole.
Her life she lives, without her true heart
for this fatuous decision, tears her apart.

All alone we both feel our hidden desire
as we're now lured, into that ring of fire.
Our love was promised in a hidden scroll
when not together, we're in a black hole.

The Love Offering

You're a pretty woman who made my head spin
with a gorgeous face, that's made like porcelain.
With long dark hair which flows down your back
such an amazing lady, who made my heart crack.

Split into two, my heart needs your lovable smile
with such voluptuous lips, I'd kiss you for a while.
Those eyes are so dark, your face does illuminate
such true elegance will make my soul regenerate.

I've never met a woman who sparkles like you do
dressed all in red; you're one lady, I must subdue.
With such a stunning figure, you're truly delicious
and the love I feel for you, becomes so auspicious.

I'd absolutely love to take you out for a nice meal
as I offer you a ring, while I crouch down to kneel.
Your one of a kind, as my heart is, a love measure
say yes to me! For our love is a heavenly treasure.

As I take you by the hand, down that narrow aisle
our hearts so excited, as we both, give out a smile.
Outside now with all our guests throwing confetti
we kiss! For our life is now guaranteed, whoopee!

You Stole My Heart

My life was simple, and really so clear
till I met you, and my heart, did cheer.
Nothing since, has remained the same
my heart now, can only see your name.

When we first met, my heart you stole
Heaven sent, our love we can't control.
Your beautiful face, I just had to adore
a lady so nice, I surely could not ignore.

I had a strange feeling, I knew you well
as though my heart, was under a spell.
I wonder, if our love was from a past life
maybe it was, and you had been my wife.

This pretty lady, with the lovely dark hair
hazel eyes, and lips so red they ensnare.
I'll love, obey and honour, for all eternity
she is the one, our hearts are now in unity.

So all I have left, to say to you my sweet
you are my life, my one true heartbeat.
You're my ray of sunshine and ray of hope
without you my darling, I cannot cope.

Valentine Princess

Well it's Valentine's Day and my heart needs you
I love you so much, I would give my life, it's true!
Valentine, Valentine my life does need you now!
You are my one true love; I need to make a vow.

Woman of my Dreams! Is a lovely thing to say to you
and a lovely poem that I wrote, especially for you!
Valentine, Valentine you are the lady I really adore
I can't say a lot, as my heart does yearn for more.

You are my guiding light, that makes my heart shine
I would certainly love, for you to be my Valentine.
My sweet, the last time we spoke, you already knew
you asked a few questions, and I nearly did tell you.

Valentine, Valentine you are my one true inspiration
so here right now! I will give you my love dedication.
Please be my Valentine and one true love, oh Yes!
I will give you all my love, my heart I now profess.

Oh Yes, Jee Yes, you are my Valentine Princess
Oh Yes, Jee Yes, I love you so much I guess
Oh Yes, Jee Yes, my heart I do Profess
Oh Yes, Jee Yes, please! Be my Valentine Princess

Love Story

I wish to write a story, about my true delight
she is the perfect woman a beauty shining bright.

I really do adore her she really does have grace
with so much sophistication, oh! And a lovely face.

She really is so gorgeous I can't believe my eyes
with her intellect and sparkling nature she really is star prize.

It really would be delightful, if she were my wife
but all that I could offer, is my heart, my soul, my life.

I have no idea why I fell for you, and really never will
the only thing that I really know is that you are so brill.

There is no other person who could ever challenge you
nothing can compare to a woman so just and true.

My heart it is breaking I'm feeling rather blue
Cupid's arrow needed, to make me appeal to you.

All my hopes and wishes can never let it pass
now I can be certain I'll never get the lass.

You're so beautiful

You're so beautiful my heart beats like a drum
I cannot resist; I fall on my knees and succumb.
Never have I met, a woman as pretty as you are
nothing can compare to you, you're a real superstar.

Everything about you makes me feel so weak
you are so lovely and charming, you're truly unique.
There isn't a single part of you that I don't adore
all I see is an attractive lady, I need more and more.

Through your eyes, I see your soul isn't surprised
that the love I have for you, is surely synchronized.
When you look at me, I can see the passion within
my love you see, that you really wish would begin.

A voice as sweet as yours is like music in my ears
I would do anything you ask, without any cheers.
Those luscious lips, that I would really like to kiss
when you open them up, oh heaven, that's bliss!

So why does our love, seem to hide from our fate
when both of us seem, to wish for it to escalate?
We can only answer this question from deep within
then maybe, just maybe, our love can then begin.

I do realize that you have probably guessed, jee yes!
All you need to do right now is make me just confess.
Remember this! That the eyes always tell the truth
look into my eyes, and you will see the proof.

Song of Love

I sing this song to you my sweet
your heart I love, it is so neat.
My love for you is what you want
come to me my pretty confidante.

Your heart it does, beat for me
my heart Is yours, I am in glee.
Our hearts together do beat as one
now that our love, has surely won.

Come with me and join in the song
our love together will always belong.
With you my love, forever alongside
we'll no right then, our love is tied.

I sing this song to you my treasure
you really are the perfect pleasure.
I know right now that you're the one
who fills my life with so much fun.

Sing with me!

Our love is joy, yes!
Our love is joy, oh! Yes!
Our love is joy, it brings me bliss
Ohhhh! Yes! Yes! Yes!

Our love is joy, our love is joy
please give me, a lovely kiss!
Our love is joy, our love is joy.
Ohhhh Yes! Yes! Yes!

Why! Oh why!

I don't really understand this love from above
why! Oh why! Can our hearts not just love?
My heart is truly yours and your heart is mine
so why! Oh why! Can't they surely combine?

When you're not there, I will really miss you
I'll be so sorry not to see that beauty, so true.
Jeez yes, I'm in love with you! My lovely darling!
Please, don't leave my heart sad and sobbing.

My heart is so on fire, it has broken in two
what can I do now? I am so in love with you.
You're leaving my heart in a right old mess
before you do depart, open up and confess.

I only have one way, to say, I love you my dear
and those are the words I write, for you to hear.
My heart is stuck on you, like some kind of glue
there really isn't a thing, I wouldn't do for you.

I have never felt so taken over by a lady before
the glamour that you have, is really top drawer.
You are such a beautiful woman, inside and out
that my heart and soul, are left without a doubt.

I really am so alive when you're around me
my heart does open up, and I look with glee.
Please let me know your true feelings soon
for I can't live without your beautiful tune.

I don't really understand this love from above
why! Oh why! Can our hearts not just love?
My heart is truly yours and your heart is mine
so why! Oh why! Can't they surely combine?

Love Inspiration

Inspiration, inspiration, my hearts true fascination
only one person does truly give, all my illumination.

Without your love, my poems, are just a nightmare
it's you that brings out, their true beauty and flare.

You're so beautiful, no one really knows you as I
nothing will stop you singing, that wonderful lullaby.

My heart and soul are lost in your hearts, sweet tune
all I need, is for our love to certainly begin very soon.

The truth has been shown; it is surely now up to you
no matter what, I'll always be there for you, it's true.

Inspiration, Inspiration, my guiding star is always right
please don't stop, and turn that bright light into night.

Now my inspiration, my hearts delight, she will ignite
fire the passion in my soul, and rescue my love plight.

Our hearts will always be together, irrelevant of today
the love we share from past lives, will never fade away.

Listen to Your Soul

The only thing I wish for in my life
is for you to be, my beautiful wife.
Our hearts and souls are in a void
wonder why, our love is so devoid.

A heart that beats in time with mine
why! Oh why, can we both not align?
I certainly need your love this day
I know it's hard, but we'll be okay!

Open your heart, to see the truth
listen in; it'll give you all the proof.
Your inner self, has already spoken
time to send, that true love token.

Look into your soul and you will see
there's lots of love for you and me.
Open those eyes, you can't ignore
that true love, you've seen before.

A previous life, when we were united
I wonder now, if your hearts excited.
Maybe this life was not meant to be
so open your heart, we'll test it see.

Then we'll know if it's Heaven sent
whether our love, was pure intent.
Listen to your soul; hidden therein
the answer does lie, deep within!

Your Eyes of True Love

The sun is out, and really shining
I'm so in love, I'm surely whining.
I love a lady; who is real stunning
my heart now, is truly humming.

Such beauty I see, within her face
and a lovely heart, so full of grace.
My mind is stuck; within your love
all I can do, is ask God up above.

You light up my life, with true glee
then bring out the best, within me.
My soul will always be, by your side
I do love you, many times I've cried.

I'll surely faint if you say, I love you
so amazed! I'd think it was untrue.
You're the sparkle, from my desire
such a beauty, puts my soul on fire.

I so need a kiss and cuddle of you
my heart in tears, my eyes of dew.
The love your heart first let show
now does hide, but I can't let go.

Why! Show me those loving eyes
the look of love, that did surprise.
You made it clear, to me that day
as your eyes with mine, did stay.

So I ask you now, please tell me!
Let me know! I'm begging thee!
Your heart is showing, you as well
its plea to you, is Tell! Tell! Tell!

Pink Heart

Let there be light, in your heart tonight
the love for me there, is ever so bright.
Don't let the darkness, engulf your soul
seek the brightness, true love your goal.

A sparkle in your brown eyes, did ignite
all the passion in me, you see each night.
You made the first move, with that wink
3 times a twinkle, and then you'd blink.

I love you, is what you have tried to say
many times, when you've come my way.
For some reason shyness, keeps us apart
when our love, is for each other's heart.

We both know Chaos, will cause us pain
you hide your love, rather than explain.
I don't understand why you do; conceal
a love so true, it's certainly the real deal.

My love, I will always be honest and true
this heart of mine, has always loved you.
Your heart, will forever be a piece of me
for there is only the love, I have for thee.

This day, I give a special message to you
from Angels of Heaven, who told me to.
Pink Heart, is a message to let you know
a man in your dream, is this man. Hello!

My Fair Lady

My fair lady dark hair down her back
her skirt is short, her tights are black.
A nice white blouse makes her sweet
a gorgeous woman, so cute and neat.

Eyes of gold that show all her emotion
oh my darling! You've got my devotion.
You look so stunning I'm so engrossed
my heart is yours, true love diagnosed.

Well! My fair lady you caught my sight
I do wish to be, your pure white knight.
I would battle against anything for you
a loyalty so true, as my heart you slew.

What can I say about such a sweet face
your eyes are amazing and full of grace.
A nose as perfect as an artist's sculpture
cheeks that glow, you're a real scorcher.

A magnificent woman who does delight
my bride I hope, in a gown of pure white.
Her hair so dark all her beauty stands out
my eyes adore, I do! I do! I do! I shout!

Secret Love

A beautiful lady with lovely dark eyes
she hides a secret, behind a disguise.
Her hair is gorgeous, so long and dark
she looks so nice, such a radiant spark.
Her pretty face, does shine and excite
she's so curvacious, a ravishing delight.

What is her secret? We'd like to know
a love so strong, her heart does glow.
She's found a love, everyone wishes for
the one true love, her heart can adore.
She hides the truth, from all her mates
both have partners; it's up to the Fates.

I've seen the twinkle as she walks past
a glimmer in the eye, my heart aghast.
I know her true love, is certainly for me
she knows my heart, does surely agree.
We just wait for the Fates, to intervene
instead of allowing, our love to be seen.

Instead of hiding those loving emotions
we should state our true love, devotions.
If those true feelings are kept in the dark
this love we share, will never ever spark.
So what we must do now! Is let it all out
open our mouths, and Scream and Shout.

Love Hope

I yearn and pray for that beautiful day
my eyes do open, my heart a bouquet.
This love I find so captivating and kind
improve my soul and expand my mind.

Chaos and Fate have hold of my heart
Cupid's arrow hits just like a love dart.
A woman I see has taken over my soul
she is my life and my heart's love goal.

I shout her name out to Heaven above
my Lord, this woman I surely now love.
I hear a voice calling back down to me
you're right, her love is surely for thee.

Proof is what my heart and soul desire
please God! Send me a heavenly choir.
A sign of love I need from my admired
so our true love, can then be acquired.

There's nothing more I want in this life
just this woman, as my delightful wife.
At night her face is forever in my head
in the morning, I hope! Our love is said.

Pop the Question

Chill out! For this evening I've planned
a nice quiet bath, and a night so grand.
A lovely evening with a woman I adore
the utmost thing, I could truly wish for.

We meet at this bar as we had agreed
a lovely chat and drink, as we proceed.
Moving to the restaurant, for our meal
she's such a lovely lady, soon I'll reveal.

As we sit at our peaceful table for two
my heart does pound for what I will do.
Champagne I order for us both to drink
my heart still pounding, will she think!

A quintet of musicians now at our table
I kneel next to her, I'm feeling unstable.
A box I open up, as she smiles with glee
my magnificent lady, please! Marry me.

She looks at me with her fabulous eyes
yes! Yes I will! She says, as she replies!
As I gaze in awe at my lady so exquisite
she kisses me, and says parents to visit.

Our Love is Pure

Eyes real blue my heart loves you
enter my soul, and now were two.
Long blonde hair that truly shines
a lady so fair, my soul just whines.

I love you so much, I certainly do
my heart is yours, my love is true.
Big blue eyes that shine with glee
I know your heart is purely for me.

Please let me know how you feel
don't ignore the love you conceal.
Reveal your passion and jubilation
and send me your love dedication.

I see you tremble when I walk past
my heart feels humble, and aghast.
As I look at you I'm in so much awe
you're perfect, I really can't ignore.

My heart is yours forever and ever
our love is pure, a joy and a pleasure.
My heart definitely needs your soul
open up and let our love be whole.

She'll Never Know

A beautiful face with so much grace
a gorgeous lady, I have to embrace.
Those hazel eyes that open my heart
a wonderful woman, she is so smart.

She's dressed like a model of delight
a short black skirt, my heart in plight.
A cute white blouse made from lace
a charming lady! My heart does race.

Her lips are coloured with bright red
I love her so much, she's in my head.
My mind is perplexed as I feel so sick
my heart is lost to this stunning chick.

She is so perfect with a body so curvy
legs so long, she does make me nervy.
I wish I could disclose my love to her
but I am foolish and my mind is a blur.

She's the most alluring lady I've seen
I do need help, God please intervene.
I am too shy for my feelings to show
she'll never know, she'll never know.

Pursuit of Love

Lovely long hair and eyes of gold
tall and slender, my heart is sold.
Just like an angel a heart so pure
a natural lady, the animals adore.

My eyes saw you and I just knew
my heart pounding, I do love you.
When I looked deep in your eyes
I saw a look, of awe and surprise.

You were amazed as much as me
so I know this love, is perfect see.
You love me as much as I love you
our hearts know, this love is true.

I can only see the wonderful you
for everything I see, I do love too.
I can't see a thing that I don't like
for you're so cute, I can't dislike.

This heart of mine loves you true
nothing will stop my love for you.
I will keep pursuing until the end
till our love, you do comprehend.

Robert Worrall

Why Do You Ignore Our Love

My perfect lady! sweet, sweet lady
why! Oh why! Do you ignore our love.
Ohh my lady! sweet, sweet, cute lady
why! Oh why! Do you ignore our love.

I know you love me, ever so true
so why do you make it, a love taboo!
I know this love is your only dream
I'd love to make, your heart scream.

I love you so much, I can't lose hope
please don't hide, as I just can't cope.
My sweet lovely woman, that I adore
send your love to me, for evermore.

Your heart of gold matches those eyes
show your heart, don't wear a disguise.
Let out that love, you desperately need
for this love of ours, we both must heed.

Forever lonely, is what I'll be without you
your my lady, I guess you know that too.
Our hearts certainly do, need each other
send out your heart, to me your lover.

My perfect lady! sweet, sweet lady
why! Oh why! Do you ignore our love.
Ohh my lady! sweet, sweet, cute lady
why! Oh why! Do you ignore our love.

Unlucky in Love

I can't find love, and I can't find happiness
Heaven's locked me out, from all this bliss.
No matter what I try, the Heavens don't do
wish or prayer! Nothing is there, just a clue!

I look around for a stunning five leaf clover
that I can't find! As luck just passes me over.
I have a lucky charm given to me by a friend
it doesn't work, so I just dream and pretend.

I have no money, and certainly no true love
for all I ever get, is trouble sent from above.
My heart is lonely, for the woman I care for
but! As all my luck, I'll cry, and she'll ignore.

What can I do to turn this bad luck to good?
I surely don't know! I just feel like firewood.
I try a spell, to help me with my loving heart
it backfires, as she has another counterpart.

I know she loves me just as much as I do her
but I have no luck, for our love to really purr.
She'll keep ignoring all those signs she sees
Heaven does bring me, down onto my knees.

I plead with Heaven, to give me one chance
as all I can get, isn't romance! Just a glance.
I look upon the skies and ask God for a sign
to say she loves me, our love will entwine.

One Day Our Love We'll Embrace

Cute and petite, you're beautiful and neat
a little curvacious, you're surely complete.
Lovely brown eyes and hair short and dark
for I'm in love with you, you ignited a spark.

With a shiny glowing darkish skin to adore
I certainly wish! Your heart I could explore.
You're smart and funny as well as amazing
a sweet woman, who I'm forever praising.

The clothes you wear are usually so bright
they show your glamour, you are a delight.
I look out for you whenever you're around
as I love you so much, my heart you found.

The name you have stands out in a crowd
as the number four, does make you proud.
The first time I saw you I did a double take
who is this woman! My dreams are awake.

You looked so pretty my eyes we're glued
what a fabulous woman! My heart is slued.
Every week I can see your sensational face
my dream, one day our love we'll embrace.

True Love Treasure

You're swift, blonde, seductive and fine
a wonder woman, who can write rhyme.
Those eyes of yours are blue like the sea
you hypnotize my heart, you're so lovely.
I sing, and dream, for a lady love like you
amazing red lips, please! A kiss would do.

So slender and tall, a model you could be
with sensational looks, I'm your devotee.
Anything you ask me, I would certainly do
for the woman I love, my pure honeydew.
You're sweet, you're pretty, and you sing
a woman like you, can do nearly anything.

I'd really like to sing a song of love to you
but! I'm not musical, you'd laugh and boo.
With a cutesy smile you light up my heart
as those hypnotic eyes, hit me with a dart.
You're the one my soul has been awaiting
for a magical love, our hearts are creating.

Thirteen is the number of our special love
and was sent to you, by a pure white dove.
Your pretty face does illuminate my desire
and then ignites my heart, it's now on fire.
A thousand lifetimes we've been together
my gorgeous angel, my true love treasure.

Love's Fairy Help

As I walk thinking only of you
I walk into a forest, to renew.
I hope and wish for your love
when I look, to see up above.

I see a forest fairy up in a tree
sprinkles her dust, all over me.
What was this for? I say to her
"ask a woman, you do prefer!"

"She wishes for you, each day
as her love does not, go away.
Her wish was sent over to me
and now! I've helped her plea".

I continue my walk in the wild
as I notice a rabbit just smiled.
Is it reality, or am I in a dream
I do know, my love is supreme.

I'm suddenly back at the road
with a heart, in love overload.
As I arrive back from my walk
there's a note to call, and talk.

A message sent from my love
with a fairy, attached thereof.
I call around as she has asked
as our love, is now unmasked.

We Are Complementary

I walk in the mountains and valleys of life
there isn't a rainbow, just pain and strife.
I love a woman, who certainly knows I do
as her hazel eyes, did shine into mine too.
She looks at me, with a sweet loving gaze
but won't admit, as she's, really in a daze.

I relax at a mountain whose name is bliss
wishing and praying, for a wonderful kiss.
As I sit and think I look to the skies above
its hazy up here, with nothing about love.
As I close my eyes I can see a lovely smile
now she's my lady, this woman with style.

While I'm there alone, a being talks to me
I can hear this voice, but no one can I see.
"Listen to your heart, the truth lies within
this lady true love, waits for you, her yin".
What does this mean? Did I have a bang?
"No! But this lady is, certainly your yang".

My mind changes to, how do I get down!
"I'll help you!" as I'm back on the ground.
Well! That was spiritual and very strange
really enlightening and nice for a change.
I'm back home and thinking quite intently
opposites attract, we are complementary.

Time to Tell

You've left my soul all broken
with the lies, you sure did tell.
Those eyes of yours all showy
as this love did, yell! Yell! Yell!

Your heart you showed to me
and your eyes sparkled to tell.
I unlocked my heart with glee
as our love did, yell! Yell! Yell!

This true love, we both found
that the Heavens did, foretell.
As my heart started to pound
all my love did, yell! Yell! Yell!

I gave everything over to you
as our hearts do perfectly gel.
But you said; it's just not true
Even if you do, yell! Yell! Yell!

Please open your loving heart
just let your love out, and tell.
For our love, must surely start
call out my love yell! Yell! Yell!

Now I have a pain in the neck
as you pretend, with your life.
Now my life is an utter wreck
time for you to, tell! Tell! Tell!

We Will Be Together

Now! I'm a man, with a poem for a heart
who's so in love, with a woman so smart.
Her long dark hair is shiny and well kept
with a face so cute, my heart really leapt.

I can see her face now, in my mind's eye
such a beauty, that she surely can't deny.
Her eyes of gold which sparkle with mine
truly amazing; they bring our souls in line.

Her soft unlit skin dazzles me with beauty
as her voice then, will leave me like putty.
She truly is, the woman of many lifetimes
as I hope and wish, we'll here bell chimes.

I would literally do anything for my adored
including give my life, without any reward.
I wish one day soon she'll open her heart
then the love we share, will certainly start.

This poem of love that I've written to you
I surely hope, does show all my heart too.
As your heart now will be with me forever
passing through time, we will be together.

Just Remember

Just Remember, I love you, ohh so much
Just Remember, I need your loving touch.
Just Remember, I wish you were my bride
Just Remember, my heart is lonely inside.

As I know! That you love me, ohh so true
and I love you, just as much as you do
Ohhh Yes! My love is just for you
as my heart, is yours forever, it's true.

Oh Just Remember, please go out with me
Just Remember, I'm sending out my plea.
Just Remember, I love you, ohh so much
Just Remember, I need your loving touch.

As I know! That you love me, ohh so true
and I love you, just as much as you do
Ohhh Yes! My love is just for you
as my heart, is yours forever, it's true.

So yes! Will you please now marry me
so then, Yesss, our hearts can forever be.
Ohhh Yes, please do let me know
Just Remember, how much you love me so.

As I know! That you love me, ohh so true
and I love you, just as much as you do
Ohhh Yes! My love is just for you
as my heart, is yours forever, it's true.

Just Remember, I love you, ohh so much
Just Remember, I need your loving touch.
Ohhh Yes! I wish you were my bride
Ohhh Yes! Stop! The loneliness inside!

Why do I love her so?

I see a beautiful lady with a dark complexion
whose beauty astounds, as she is perfection.
Her long dark hair, makes her truly desirable
such a wonderful face, it makes me excitable.

With her eyes of honey so pure they astound
my heart is racing, for a stunning lady I found.
Her lips are luscious as they glisten in the light
her clothes are glamorous, and ever so bright.

The rainbow of colours, which she does wear
bring out her beauty, as my love, I do declare.
She's definitely faultless with curves just right
my heart and soul are lost, as she's dynamite.

I know my prospects are really none existent
but the desire I have, is absolutely consistent.
Every time I close my eyes, I see her cute face
for a fabulous woman as this, does have grace.

I've wished for her love so many times before
my heart is crumbling, and she shuts the door.
What do I have without the woman I do adore
nothing but pain, as I need her so much more!

I look up to the sky and ask for a helping hand
but nothing is there, why! I don't understand.
How can I love a woman who just ignores me!
Why do I love her so? Because she loves me!

We'll Tie The Knot

I wake up in the morning, and look outside
is this life for real, and was it, prophesized.
Why am I here? And what is my life about?
Am I human? And will I always have doubt?

I seek answers to so many tough questions
maybe there's no ideas, or any suggestions.
As I turn within my own heart, to find space
I write a poem, to create a time and a place.

I've always known a true love is what I seek
since I was born, to this moment, and week.
No matter what I do it never does transpire
my feelings say; it will happen as you desire.

I do have faith in what will happen in my life
but I can't stop thinking; true love, not strife.
Even now I query! Why do I love her so true
inside a voice says: She really does love you!

Do allow the universe to alter things you ask
for this is why it did arise, to aid in your task.
As Heaven has a plan for you, and everyone
and the true love you ask, she loves you hun.

Now I know my life's goal is a true love quest
as for all those other queries, later addressed.
At this moment in time I need to concentrate
for this true love quest, as I must sit and wait.

My life is so much happier, for Heaven's plan
and one day my love she'll be, and I her man.
It' doesn't matter if her love is hidden or not
for she knows, deep down, we'll tie the knot.

True Love's Key

One day our hearts will really decay,
but true love survives so that's okay.
I know, as I've had the premonitions
so many times, with so many visions.

This woman I see, does hold the key
a key to our love, which she can see.
Her eyes do shine, like a crystal gold
they're the key which she does hold.

The lock for the key is poetry by me
with those eyes she'll read, and see.
When lock and key, are turned right
our pure true love, we'll both recite.

This poetry of love, she does peruse
for she can spot, those hidden clues.
She has put the key, in a poetry lock
as she turns it, our love she'll unlock.

As the One you did foresee this time
as you do read these poems of mine.
Your hazel eyes, unlock our devotion
for our true love, is poetry in motion.

Love Plea

I'm so unhappy I feel like I'm going mad
my heart is all alone, and my soul is sad.
As I love a woman who hides her desire
and leaves my heart, completely on fire.

All I have is my wishes and these words
as I sit and listen, to the cute little birds.
Outside, the sun is glowing with delight
while my heart burns, with a love plight.

So sad and lonely, my heart is yearning
while my soul, does feel like its burning.
My eyes so bloodshot are ever so teary
as my desires, have now gone all weary.

This love for her will always be with me
and my soul does truly, need sympathy.
I hope, I pray, and wish every single day
the truth she'll say, my love is true! Ok!

My words are written, with a love plea
please! Beautiful lady, I truly love thee.
Just unleash those true feelings, inside
and our true love will then, be verified.

Once revealed, our love we can cherish
knowing deep down, it'll never perish.
The understanding, our souls have got
will bring us happiness, and a little tot.

Tears of Love

As the rain comes down, my tears do as well
I'm in love with a woman, who is really swell.
I cry and cry! Tears trickling down my cheeks
I've loved her so long, now my heart, shrieks.

I call out her name, every minute of each day
hoping and wishing, that she'll call, someday.
I live in hope, as she's my one true goal in life
for there's nothing I can do, my life's in strife.

The rain gets heavier, as the wind, now blows
as the pain in my heart, just grows and grows.
I'm truly in agony as my love is totally sincere
but as the weather, my problems are, severe.

I get an impression; she suffers the same way
from the way she spoke, before she run away.
If she'd just sit down, and have a talk with me
we could then conclude, if our love should be!

If our hearts could join, our love, would shine
then our lovely souls, would surely intertwine.
Even though she understands her love for me
the life she's now chosen, is woe, and misery!

My Secret Admirer

I've got a secret admirer who now watches me
she views me from afar, in the shadows to see.
She patiently observes, with her true affection
but lacks courage to say, as she fears rejection.

We only met recently, but her love was instant
she loves everything I do, but still keeps distant.
When she sees my eyes, her heart beats so fast
as her eyes gaze lovingly, her love is sure to last.

She is so perceptive, and understands me well
but hides her feelings, and wonders how to tell.
Use your perception and you may be surprised
for my heart is also, hidden, and kept disguised.

You hope one day I will notice your loving eyes
if you watch closely, you'll see I do sympathize.
I know you remember everything, ever so well
so keep using those eyes, then our love can gel.

The right moment is here, for you to say to me
I love you my sweet, with lingering eyes of glee.
Then whisper over to me, your true loving plea
wait till I can see and hear, and see my, yippee!

Speak to me! My Love

Her golden eyes and lovely long dark locks
took me by surprise, for this woman rocks.
Her sweet soft voice was music to my ears
I'm so enchanted, I've loved her, for years.

With a face so pretty she makes me whole
I do love her, as my heart does rock 'n' roll.
I dance around a maypole, and yell for her
for she watches me, as my heart does purr.

My eyes are glowing like the sun in the sky
for I'm in love with this woman, who's shy.
Will she make her move or will she not say
does she pick our love, or throw it all away.

She has asked her mother for some advice
and whether or not, to make that sacrifice.
Listen to your heart, your love does shout!
Don't lose a love, which is true and devout.

If you would, speak with me, I'd tell you so
along with, I do love you my heart is aglow.
Inside my heart, I know I love you so much
as I really need, your kind and loving touch.

White Soul, Cloud Soul

I walked in the Valley of Kings, for a while
with wealth and riches, and gold, in a pile.
Well! I definitely did, have a heart of gold
as I loved my wealth, but my life was cold.

With all these riches, and the power I had
my heart was empty, and my soul, all sad.
As my heart and soul are lost in the abyss
for I need true love, for my life, to be bliss.

In my early life I had found a love so pure
until power and wealth, did then obscure.
She was so beautiful, I had a statue made
to honour this lady, my life then betrayed.

What I'd give, for my true love once again
this woman so pure, who I do love, Amen!
Unfortunately, time has now passed us by
Now in another life, but! For her, I still cry!

I still search, for this woman I love so true
recently though I've found her, she knew!
The instant attraction when our eyes met
our hearts now beating, in a musical duet.

Now I've realized that you're my true Hun
as I'm a white soul, to your cloud soul one.
Yin and Yang, or opposites forever united
as our pure true love, will forever be cited.

The Unforeseen

I can see a woman's face; her glamour is exquisite
for she is the woman, my heart does desire to visit.
I do love her, but know now! It'll never materialize
as I'm all alone, wishing her love, she'd formalized.

My heart is pounding and my head is in lots of pain
as I wish and pray, I could see her now and explain.
I feel so lonely, as I need to hear her cute soft voice
my head is spinning, but I have no reason to rejoice.

I see another face, as my body feels so light and airy
it's my daughters! And she is such, a cute little fairy.
I'm feeling so sad as I left her without a hug and kiss
I hope she remembers, I do love my pretty little miss.

Well! I've seen the two most important ladies in life
but now! I'm toppling and spinning, with great strife.
Childhood and so many other events in my life, I see
this gives me pleasure and much happiness and glee.

They do say life flashes in front of you, before death
yes! I can definitely say yes! As I now hold my breath.
Bang! As my body hits the floor, at a fantastic speed
I'm no more! My body is still, and beginning to bleed.

Magpies of Love

I see a magpie in the garden looking at me
here comes another, they stare, then flee.
As I resume my writing, in the sun outside
abruptly two magpies, are back at my side.

This is very weird, as I'm feeling so scared
as I look again, they're still there! I stared!
Suddenly! I got the urge to go out instead
and go for a nice walk, and clear my head.

I walk along an old track, now overgrown
this is a usual route, today! It's unknown!
Why do I sense something amiss, this day
I wish to turn back, but can't! I must obey.

The sunlight is now so bright, ahead of me
I don't know where I'm going, I can't see!
As I move along, the sunlit track up ahead
finally! I can see, as I gaze at a lady in red!

"Help" she says, as I can sense she's hurt
"I've fallen of a horse, into that pile of dirt".
I phone for an ambulance, to help this lady
and wait till they arrive, for her own safety.

Later that week she rings to say thank you
and asks me, if I would like dinner out, too.
I say, yes, as we arrange a nice dinner date
and now we're married, such a lovely fate!

Those magpies, brought our hearts, in line
as though Fate, had used them to entwine.
Without them, we would never ever meet
now each morning, the magpies we greet!

Love Ripple

I see a raindrop land in a puddle nearby
it causes a ripple, as my heart does sigh.
Like the woman I love so pure, and true
she caused a ripple in my heart, it grew!

So many raindrops plunge in the puddle
creating circles that will kiss, and cuddle.
As I watch, a circle of true love is shown
your soul hit mine, as a raindrop thrown.

Inside the puddle a rainbow is now seen
a heavenly light, which really does glean.
As my true love is a sweet heavenly light
she makes my day, and makes, my night!

The rain pours down and I'm getting wet
it forms a sound, just like a musical duet.
My heart and soul are dancing in the rain
I love you so much, my heart you've slain.

I begin to sing with the sounds I can hear
drip drop, a crash of thunder, bang, bang.
I love you! I love you! My heart, you rang
I love you! I love you! For your love I sang.

I just sing, and sing, and dance and dance
for this love I've found, is a true romance.
So much fun I have in this rain and puddle
please! My beautiful lady, I need a cuddle.

Genie of Love

Many years ago, when the two of us first met
an old bottle did unseal, with a love, to beget.
As your eyes of gold, dazzled my eyes, of blue
the oceans surrendered, this bottle to renew.

Over the years, our love has grown and grown
this hidden bottle, then opened the unknown.
Inside was our heartfelt love, we'd had before
as this vapour will make. our love forevermore.

As soon as the genie, was released from inside
our love was sealed, as both our hearts sighed.
Never again will our love, be resealed within it
our hearts shout, our true love, will never quit.

Many lifetimes ago we created, this love genie
so our true love decree, would always, be free.
Remember your vow, this love is, your destiny
as nothing else, can bring your soul, pure Ch'i!

Our love secured in a bottle, was for pleasure
a moment of joy our love created, to treasure.
Never realizing it would come back, to help us
all that's left, is for our love, to be, beauteous.

The Hidden Chest

I find an old wooden chest; hidden up in the attic
should I open it! Or should I not!! I feel dramatic!
My heart is thumping, as I wonder, what's inside
will it still open up, or will it need a key? I sighed!
I look at the front, but can't see, a key hole at all
I open the catch, and toss the lid back to the wall.
My heart is definitely pounding, with anticipation
as I peer inside, nothing! Now that's a revelation!

The next thing I know, I'm standing there shaking
while the attic room and house are now, quaking.
"Hello there my friend" As a voice speaks so loud!
I'm trembling with fear, as I can see a white cloud.
Suddenly! I'm overwhelmed, with a weird feeling
that I should now, be bowing down, and kneeling.
"I am the voice, which sends out the word to you"
"I know your heart, and the woman you love too."

"Like this chest, your life is void, without her love
but! Lucky for you both, I'm the word from above.
I have come down, through this holy wooden ark
to help you both out, and to help your love spark.
The two of you, have been praying, up to the sky
as I've now come, to help your true love, magnify.
To open this wooden ark was your fates, destiny
enacted by a woman's love, as she cries for thee."

The lid now closes, and everything seems normal
that was really strange, and certainly paranormal.
I begin to think, it was some kind, of weird dream
until that is! I literally walk into this lady, I scream!
Our eyes meet, as we gaze lovingly, at each other
she holds my hand and says: "Please be my lover."
I whisper back to her, as I say, yes! I do love you!
She looks up to the heavens and says, Thank You!

91

A Nice Cup of Tea

I put the kettle on to make myself a cup of tea
it's so metallic and like a mirror, I can see, me!
As it now boils, steam pours out from its spout
I see my lady! My heart does steam and shout!
It's just her reflection, as she wanders past me
I've gone cherry red, as the cup I've got for tea.

I pour the water into a cup, I have made ready
wishing my love I was pouring, to you my lady.
While I'm dreaming of her, I stir inside the cup
just like my heart! Oh my! I'm a love sick, pup!
My mind does go astray, as I put some sugar in
the bubbles on the top, are kissing and cuddlin!

Now I go to get my lunch, I leave my tea there
as I return she looks at me, and offers, a chair.
I take my lunch over, and place it on the table
I sit down next to her, but I'm a little unstable.
Suddenly I remember my tea's near the kettle
so I must go over and get it, and then resettle.

I pick up the tea cup, without using the handle
Ouch! It's too hot! More like, a burning candle.
Back down! Now I see a letter left there for me
I open it, and see a heart, sent with a love plea.
As I pull out the note, I see what she's, written
It says; I love you so much, my heart is smitten.

Love Meditation

I sit down lotus style, and then close my eyes
Om Mani Bêmê Hum! Om Mani Bêmê Hum!
As I begin to meditate, on a lady that purifies
Om Mani Bêmê Hum! Om Mani Bêmê Hum!

She is my guiding light, and my one, true love
A lady who loves me, sent down, from above.
While I contemplate, the love, we both share
I can see her pretty face, as I send a love flare

Her sweet golden eyes, do enlighten, my soul
and help me concentrate, for she is in control.
I can sense our hearts beating just like a drum
a pure love alignment, Oṃ Maṇi Padme Hūṃ!

The stars will twinkle and sparkle, at our souls
for our love is destiny, as written in the scrolls.
Two opposite souls, who really do sing-a-long
you love me! I love you! Án mani bát mê hồng!

Our minds are now attached in contemplation
as our hearts create, a true love, constellation.
Look! See this light, you and me it shines upon
Heaven says; we're one!, Um ma ni pa mi hon!

Fate has formulated, this love we both desire
Om Mani Banme Hum! Om Mani Banme Hum!
As my soul and your soul are a heavenly choir.
Om Mani Banme Hum! Om Mani Banme Hum!

Love Heart

I draw a heart for the woman of my dreams
for my own heart just screams, and screams.
As I continue to sketch, I put an arrow within
just like the arrow, that made our love begin.

On one side, I draw a man dressed all in blue
on the other side, a lady, in a hazel dress too.
Your eyes are hazel and mine blue as the sea
for I love you, forever and ever, you and me!

What else can I do with this drawing of mine?
I know! I can sketch a snake, in the heart sign.
Right down the middle I put a serpentine line
as our love is infinite, and will always entwine.

Black and white, are the colours I use to unite
light and dark, yin and yang, opposites alright.
Our souls are opposites; born to interconnect
together we are, complementary and perfect.

I sketch two perfect circles around as the key
the first is to show, we're aligned for eternity.
The other is a gold ring from our wedding day
for the love I have for you, will never go away.

I've finished my drawing, and add it to a card
it has this poem inside, from your loving bard.
I put it inside an envelope sealed with my kiss
then post it to you, for our anniversary bliss!

Stone Circle of Love

I've woken up in this large, circle of stone
I'm cold and lonely, in this secluded zone.
Why did I come? And how did I get here?
I can't remember! As my mind's unclear!
It's totally silent as there's no sound at all
completely pitch-black, as its still nightfall.
I walk to the edge, and find I can't get out
there's an invisible fence, I yell and shout.

I sit down on a flat stone, to contemplate
and watch a bright light up high, navigate.
Closer and closer, this light is now getting
as my heart is pounding, and I'm, fretting.
Suddenly! There's a loud, humming noise
as I see my lady love, in a heavenly, poise.
Then I ask her; what are you doing, here?
She says; "I just don't know! I've no idea!"

She sits down as we discuss, our situation
as we're isolated, in this stone formation.
As we talk, I eventually say that I love her
she says, "I love you, my heart does purr."
We hug and kiss, under the stars up high
a stone block begins to crumble, and cry!
As we watch our names, appear in stone
here's the love vow, your souls enthrone.

Two golden rings, come from the ground
as two stars land in the rings, to astound.
A voice then says, "Your presents of love
are star rings, sent from Heaven, above."
"They'll appear when your love, you see
in the eyes, a true love ring, is your key!"
"Only you two can see the vows in stone
a circle of love, made by you two, alone!"

Sea of Tears

The truth is visible within your sweet eyes
you watch me, as your heart hits the skies.
That sparkle I see, as you look towards me
makes my own eyes blue, just like the sea.

As our eyes twinkle and dance with a glow
in an instant, our hearts in love sure know.
Your hair is gentle, and glistens like you do
my legs are shaking, I'm so in love with you.

Such beautiful dark hair, long and amazing
you're truly perfect, as I just keep, praising.
I see your face and become lost in a dream
you are so gorgeous, my eyes like a stream.

Tears of delight, for such a wonderful lady
I love you so much, my hearts, now debris.
The first time we met the sun shone on us
as I was too shy, and couldn't make a fuss.

The tears of my eyes have made an ocean
now! I can't stop, my hearts true devotion.
As I drown within these tears of pure love
I can only watch this dream, from thereof.

The ocean is so vast and a wonderful blue
as my heart is lonely, and my soul a canoe.
I paddle and row, and don't get anywhere
I need you and you need me, it's so unfair.

This love we share is kept apart, by waves
as both our hearts, surely crave and crave.
We need to be saved from our own abyss
so that our love is sealed, with a teary kiss!

Beautiful Feeling

I watch a white feather, as it drops on the ground
my angel is here, to help with this love I've found.
I pick it up, and stare up, at the sunny skies above
a cloud is forming, in the shape of a heart, of love.

What an amazing moment, to have a sign like this
a Heavenly sent message, to show, true love bliss.
My face is all smiles, as I picture this woman I love
such a beautiful feeling, Heaven has sent, thereof.

I've prayed, and prayed, for a sign, from up above
as to show her feelings, and to tell me, of her love.
All I need now is for all those feelings to be shown
so then our true love can never ever, be unknown.

Her astounding beauty, is not all of what I can see
she's so intelligent, and a love of nature, help me!
Hair so long and dark, and her eyes, are pure gold
my hearts just a mess, Lord, behold! Lord, behold!

I need her love so much, that I would do anything
I'd give her my heart and soul, in fact, everything.
With all my heart and soul, I will give you this ring
a nice little fairy ring, as our earthly, love offering.

As you find this fairy ring, a white feather, will fall
then you'll find our love, with tears, of a waterfall.
With this, your loving heart will find the fire inside
Earth, Air, Water and Fire, our love now, purified!

My Hearts, Beholden

Where is my muse? Where has she gone?
I'm certainly confused, and, I'm all alone!
My one true love, the woman of my heart
I need you hereof, so my wishes can start.

Without my muse, my soul has no energy
as you infuse my heart, with all its poetry.
Your name is a word, that gives me, hope!
This heart you stirred, my soul does mope.

Words have such beauty, within my heart
you're such a cutie, now! Where do I start!
I know you're smart, and your eyes golden
my true counterpart, my hearts, beholden.

You're names a mantra, my soul will utter
proclaims our love, our hearts now flutter.
I see your face, such beauty is astounding
my hearts apace, your love is surrounding.

A scent of roses, and our hearts combine
my muse she poses, and our hearts, align.
For she exists, and her heart, is pure gold
truth she resists, but her love, will unfold.

What must you do? Your heart, does ask
your soul is true, stop wearing that mask.
A specific word will make you, audacious
a name you slurred, our love is tenacious.

Perfect Lady

I gaze and gaze at those sweet, loving, golden eyes
my heart is simmering and my soul, you crystallize.
You hypnotize me, as I see a lady of true perfection
as you flutter those eyelashes, I see the connection.
I'm completely entranced, with your gorgeous face
I see a tenderness, that's wrapped up, in pure lace.
Hair so long and dark, it shimmers, within the light
a perfect frame, to outline a lady, who is, just right.

I'm in such a daze, I must sit down, and admire you
my heads all over the place, and my hearts just goo.
As you walk towards me, I notice, your lovely dress
oh my! I can't take anymore! I wish, you'd say, yes!
Such a slender figure, dressed so lovely, in pure red
wow! Now you're messing, with my head, my head.
You walk towards me, and give such a radiant smile
you're such a sumptuous woman, my hearts fragile.

I do look away, but! My love for you, is too, intense
as you pass by and look, my loving heart, you sense.
You glance at me as your eyes of gold, are twinkling
when all of a sudden, you stop! Now I'm crimsoning.
You sit right down beside me, and then say; "hello"
my body's trembling, as you ask me, why I'm aglow.
My words are a complete jumble, as I can't, confess
she says; "it doesn't matter, I truly love you, I guess".

Fates Love Storm

Thunder and lightning, crashing! Its bloodcurdling
darkness in the skies, as the rain comes, a lashing.
Heavy rain splashes, as the lightning, hits the roof
now I'm shaking, my lady, she can't, see the truth.

The sky ignites with each and every, lightning bolt
now my heart is thumping, as it's broken, by a jolt.
Split into two, by an arrow, so bright and in flames
the woman you love is written there, Cupid claims.

"We'll no longer watch you both being theoretical
the Fates have decided, your love will be, poetical.
This storm of Heaven, will make this love transpire
with all this thunder and lightning, it will, conspire."

"The woman you love does love you but won't say
she'll not be able to lie or hide, this won't go away.
This Heaven sent thunderstorm is on its way to her
when it's finished, only your heart, will she prefer."

"As your souls, your two hearts are interconnected
this celestial storm is a vow, your love is protected.
Time and time, we have watched your love pass by
this time! Fates super storm will, make you comply."

"Both of you will only now see each other, at night
and every waking moment, you'll be in love plight.
Two hearts and souls separated a long time before
never again! For your soul's true love, will restore!"

Secret Romance

Joy filled words, our hearts do sing
secretive love, is a wonderful thing.
Examine the soul, for romanticism
shadows expose, secret symbolism.

Lost in each other, our love is clear
opening up! Now that's a real, fear.
Venerate, don't hide from this fate
express your love, let it consecrate.

Stars in Heaven, our loves forecast
beautiful woman, my souls, aghast.
Open your heart, the truth is inside
recall your eyes gazing, as I replied.

On that first day, the sun, did shine
Heaven sent, 'twas a righteous sign.
Spiritual angels and an aura of light
opened our hearts, to a love delight.

My soul has found, this lady so pure
charming and cute, my loves secure.
Unified in love, as a knot is now tied
happily married, to my lovely, bride.

Planned Love

I have a dream that we're together, as our true love, is forever and ever.
We're happily married in my dream, and really do make, a perfect team.
Our nice house, is in the countryside, as we sit and cuddle, by the
fireside.

We love to walk amongst the trees, by animals, insects, birds and bees.
A woman of nature who is so pure, the love of my life, she's so demure.
In my dream I've seen her true soul, the love we share, makes us whole.

We meet each day the sun is good, to have a picnic, like lovers should.
We sit together as we eat our food, I gaze at her beauty, my eyes glued.
Feeling happy I'm certainly blessed, to have this woman, she's the best.

Her long dark hair shines in the sun, in a field running, we're having fun.
We sit back down for a needed rest, and gaze fondly, we're so obsessed.
She moves herself to be close to me, I kiss her lips, she's certainly for
me.

Abruptly she's gone from my dream, what have I done, I let out a
scream.
What is this! Lots and lots of books! As one falls off, one of those hooks.
It hits me hard as I look at the cover, showing me and this woman, as
my lover.

As I open the book and start to read, about my dream and the lady I
need.
I realize it's a book sent from above, to show us both, God's sent our
love.
With this, I now begin to understand, that our true love, has surely been
planned.

Pure as Lace

Knock! Knock! You're as pure as lace
Knock! Knock! With such a gorgeous face
Knock! Knock! You're my one desire
Knock! Knock! You set my heart on fire

You can't ignore the truth
that our love is pure and couth.
We both need each other
for my heart does need its lover.
So set your emotion free
don't just panic, be honest and true to me.

Ooooh, I so love you! Yes I do!

Knock! Knock! You're as pure as lace
Knock! Knock! With such a gorgeous face
Knock! Knock! You're my one desire
Knock! Knock! You set my heart on fire

I really need your loving heart
as you're hearts tearing mine apart.
For this love I have for you, is ever so true
and my heart is only for you!
I wish you could be my bride
dressed in white, Oh my! I sighed!

Ooooh, I so love you! Yes I do!

Knock! Knock! You're as pure as lace
Knock! Knock! With such a gorgeous face
Knock! Knock! You're my one desire
Knock! Knock! You set my heart on fire

Pure as Lace (Cont.)

All dressed in satin white
a beautiful woman whose dynamite.
With eyes of sparkling gold
my love for you is now unrolled.
Our hearts are one and the same
I'd shout it to the world, I've no shame!

Ooooh, I so love you! Yes I do!

Knock! Knock! You're as pure as lace
Knock! Knock! With such a gorgeous face
Knock! Knock! You're my one desire
Knock! Knock! You set my heart on fire

When this love begins
hopefully!
We'll have some twins.
Living a life with so much ecstasy
as our true love
is pure fantasy.

Ooooh, I so love you! Yes I do!

Knock! Knock! You're as pure as lace
Knock! Knock! With such a gorgeous face
Knock! Knock! My bride soon to be
Knock! Knock! I do! Honour, Love
and Obey Thee

Ooooh, I so love you! Yes I do!

ABOUT THE AUTHOR

This is me, Robert Worrall you see
the one who writes, all this poetry.
I am a poet, and photograph taker
historian, and a museum curator.

I come from Congleton, in Cheshire
but now, in Biddulph, Staffordshire.
I was born, during the month of June
evening birth, and a waning moon.

I write my poems; mainly about love
sometimes with help, from up above.
My soul will help, my poems endure
so then my heart, can seek the pure.

I hope you all, enjoy the things I write
and that it gives, a little bit of delight.
I hope you keep, reading all my poetry
that they bring hope, and a bit of glee.

Printed in Great Britain
by Amazon